T0104339

Presented to:

By:

"These are the truths I want deep in my children's hearts, as well as my own! With lyrical lines and beautiful illustrations, Melissa explains the concept of grace in a way that's memorable and easy to understand for children. It's so catchy, you'll find yourself chanting the lines all throughout your day."

**Laura Wifler**, co-founder of Risen Motherhood

"A delightful way to unpack the grace of God with the kids in your life—it makes deep truths accessible for young and not so young hearts alike."

**Ruth Chou Simons**, author, artist, and founder of gracelaced.com

"Melissa offers big truths to small people in a book that will both teach and delight. Here is a message of grace-covered failures and grace-fueled obedience that bears repeating, for children and parents alike. Good news for all from cover to cover."

**Jen Wilkin**, author and Bible teacher

"A lovely explanation of God's grace that every child (and grown-up!) can understand."

**Bob Hartman**, Bible storyteller and songwriter

"The adorable illustrations, the rhyming words, and the relatability of this book make it easier for me as a parent to explain and embrace the vastness of God's grace in my five-year old's everyday life. It is delightful!"

**Quina Aragon**, mother and author

# HIS
# GRACE
# IS ENOUGH

Written by

## Melissa Kruger

Illustrated by

## Isobel Lundie

thegoodbook
for children

His Grace Is Enough
© Melissa Kruger / Isobel Lundie 2022. Reprinted 2022.

"The Good Book For Children" is an imprint of The Good Book Company Ltd
thegoodbook.com | thegoodbook.co.uk | thegoodbook.com.au | thegoodbook.co.nz | thegoodbook.co.in

Illustrated by Isobel Lundie | Art direction and design by André Parker

ISBN: 9781784987510 | Printed in India

Oh, don't run away
Come sit over here
Let's talk together
You've nothing to fear

I've something important
  To tell you today
It's **TRUE** and it's **HOPEFUL**
  And helps guide your way

God's grace is enough
  It's so **BIG** and so **FREE**
His grace is enough
  Both for **YOU** and for **ME.**

If you make a
# BIG MESS

Or tell a
## SMALL LIE

If you're lazy with chores
And don't even TRY

If you get

# FIERY MAD

And hit someone hard

Or **CHEAT** a good friend
As you play in the yard

If you **STEAL** someone's toy
Or say something **MEAN**
What can you do
To make yourself clean?

Running and hiding
Away from the light—
Will that be enough
To make it all right?

I'll tell you again
   For you need to know
**NEVER** forget this
   Wherever you go...

God's grace is enough
   It's so **BIG** and so **FREE**
His grace is enough
   Both for **YOU** and for **ME.**

You might try to hide
By doing what's good
**TRYING** to fix it—
If only you could!

Make **STRAIGHT A**s in school
And never complain

Not even when lunch is **SOAKED** by the rain

You try and you try
You try hard as you might
Will that be **ENOUGH**
To make it all right?

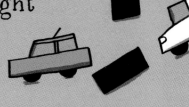

My child, here's the truth
From God, you **CAN'T HIDE**
He sees what you've done
He knows what's **INSIDE**

But please don't despair
There's good news, I say!
Whatever you do
**GOD'S GRACE**
makes a way

Yes, his grace is enough
It's so **BIG** and so **FREE**
His grace is enough
Both for **YOU** and for **ME.**

Here's how it works:
Jesus died on the cross
**WE** gain new life
Because **HE** suffered loss

Though we don't deserve it
Our God is **SO KIND**
That's grace pure and simple
The **BEST** thing to find

So just say you're sorry
It's **AMAZING**, you see

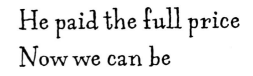

He paid the full price
Now we can be

# FREE!

Not free to sin more
He doesn't want that
Free to **LIVE FREE**
And that's a great fact

Believing in Jesus
He gives a new heart

And **FORGIVES**
all our sin
So **NEW LIFE**
can start

So there's no need
to **HIDE**
And no need to **RUN**

Now you can
serve him with

**GLADNESS**

**AND FUN**

I love you **SO MUCH**
I want you to know
Cling to this truth
Wherever you go...

His grace is enough...

To change you and
change me.